3:01 P.M. PACIFIC WAR TIME

A Photographic Memoir
Victory in Europe

Emil Edgren, Official Photographer
US Army, World War II

As told to Gale Geurin

AuthorHouse™
1663 Liberty Drive
Bloomington, IN 47403
www.authorhouse.com
Phone: 1-800-839-8640

First published by AuthorHouse 3/25/2011

ISBN: 978-1-4520-8075-8 (sc)

Library of Congress Control Number: 2010914596

All photographs in **3:01 P.M. Pacific War Time** *are the sole property of Emil Edgren,*
and any production is strictly by permission of the author.

Printed in the United States of America

This book is printed on acid-free paper.

authorHOUSE®

DEDICATION

This book is dedicated to
the thousands of American soldiers
buried in a foreign lands,
never to return home.

These young men,
most in their late teens or early twenties,
are the unsung heroes,
many of heroic deeds we may never know
To each, we owe a debt of gratitude
for their ultimate sacrifice
that we, the world,
could enjoy freedom and liberty..

Emil Edgren is a renowned photographer, whose friends and contemporaries included Joe Rosenthal and Ernie Pyle. Emil was in Paris when General deGaulle announced the end of the war in Europe. He caught that exact moment with his camera. "*3:01 P.M. Pacific War Time*," is an exhibition of moment-in-time photographs taken following that historic moment in time when the War in Europe was declared over, showing the French citizenry, American military, and scenes of recovery. In addition to his wartime experiences, Emil's impressive resume includes:

Emil Edgren, US Army Official Camerman
World War II
Paris 1945

San Francisco Art Institution, state scholarship contest.
United States Army Pictorial Service, 4 ½ years
San Francisco Studio, Self-Employed, 5 years
    (advertising and fashion)
International News Photos, 2 years, contracted photojournalist
Associated Press, 1 year, contracted photojournalist
United Press International, 10 years contracted photojournalist
    – covered the 1962 Olympics
San Francisco Call Bulletin, 10 years staff photojournalist
San Francisco Examiner, 1 year staff photojournalist
San Jose Mercury News, 20 years, staff photojournalist,
    retired assistant chief photographer.
San Francisco Bay Area Press Photographer's Association,
    Lifetime member,*Capitola Museum Board*, former member
Capitola Arts Commission, Member

Recognition and Awards

Letter of commendation, Herb Shannon,
    World War II, 82nd Airborne, Battle of the Bulge
International Photographic Exposition,
    first place color category
United Press International, 1973,
    national photograph of the month
Santa Clara County Fair 1962,
    first place, black, black and white category
City and Mayor of San Jose Commendation 1987
Permanent display of Almaden Valley photographs,
    Almaden Library and Community Center

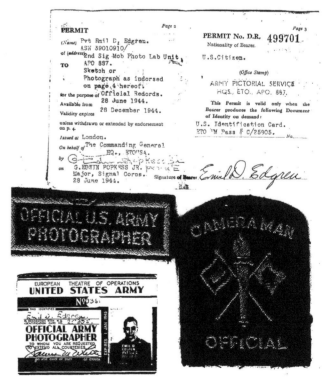

Emil Edgren, Official U.S. Army Photographer: These are the
credentials which Cpl Emil Edgren carried during WWII.

3:01 P.M.
PACIFIC WAR TIME

A Photographic Memoir
Victory in Europe

Emil Edgren, Official Photographer
US Army, World War II

PARIS. May 8, 1945. Standing in the middle of Plaza de la Bastille in Paris, one could almost hear the ghostly echo of guns, and the shouts of the SS herding suspected underground sympathizers to shadowy places from which they never returned. The reality of the day had not yet been completely absorbed by the Parisians coming to the plaza. The anticipated announcement was still minutes off as slowly they came, hesitantly at first, hoping it was true while at the same time unbelieving that it could be. One by one, then in twos and families, parents grasping the sweaty hands of their children, they begin to gather, facing the imposing edifice of the Academie Nationale de Musique *(National Music Academy).*

At precisely 3:01 p.m. Pacific War Time, the voice of French General deGaulle boomed over the large speakers mounted on the outside of the famous opera house. "The war in Europe is ended. Germany has surrendered. Viva la France!"

It was at that moment in time that I, as an official Army photographer, swept the plaza with my camera and caught the clock in my lens. 3:01 p.m. The square was full, and the announcement was met with a collective holding of breath as though the world stood still. Then the cheers began. Hats were tossed into the air, men and women hugged each other, and some stood still and looked up where the blue skies over Paris were empty of enemy planes. The cheers and shouts merged together until the Plaza de la Concorde vibrated with the triumphant roar.

Paris May 8 1945, Opera House at 3:01 Pacific War Time

This is the photographic memory of that time and place, when the world emerged from its years of imprisonment and world-wide war, and men and women could walk in Paris again without fear, without looking over their shoulders for the dreaded Nazis. Men could talk again freely about anything without fearing their words would be used against them.

The gathering in Paris stretched for miles from the plaza to the Arch of Triumph, to Napoleon's Tomb and Norte Dame Cathedral. In less than an hour there was standing room only, and stand they did . . . on street lamps, on trucks, on statuary, on balconies, on each other. It was a time of celebration, the like of which no one in France had thought would come.

GI on pole in Iceland

This is the indelible history of that day, of what followed, of the freedom all now expect, but few could believe on historical afternoon of **May 5, 1945 at precisely 3:01 p.m. Pacific War Time.**

It had been a long journey from being a kid in San Francisco to photographing Generals Eisenhower, Bradley and deGaulle in Paris on that day in 1945 when the war in Europe was officially over.

Four years earlier, in 1941 before the infamous attack on Pearl Harbor, I had graduated high school and decided to put in one year in the Army before settling down. That would be my patriotic duty and save me from the draft. We weren't officially at war then, but there were rumors it wouldn't be long before our country joined England in combating the Nazi hoard that was storming across Europe. My interest in photography began long before that, and what piqued my interest in the Army was the promise by the recruiter that I would attend the Army pictorial school in New Jersey. That seemed ideal . . . having the government pay for the school that I could not afford and, after a year of obligatory duty, I would have the know-how and experience to open my own studio. I kissed my girl Lucille good-bye and told her I'd return in a year. She promised to wait. It was a win-win situation.

Lucille

Unlike Lucille, recruiter promises are like feathers in the wind, blown away before one could snatch one. With the photo school full, I was offered an "aerial photography school," which I declined because, quite frankly, it didn't seem to have any after-the-Army potential. I held out for photography school. After all, I was promised it, and recruiters didn't lie. Did they?

After basic training at Ft. Ord, California, and assigned to the 54th Signal Battalion in California, I was still chaffing that I hadn't been selected for photo school when our group was suddenly, and without warning, ordered to the Philippines.

Ft Ord

December 7, 1941, our ship headed across the ocean toward the Philippines and visions of dancing girls in grass skirts and sunny beaches filled my head. This was a plum assignment, and, as a matter of fact, the code name for our destination was "Plum," which goes to show that even the Army had a fine sense of humor.

Our ships were unescorted out there on the balmy Pacific that bright Sunday morning. With American flags flying in the breeze, and bigger, brighter ones painted across the sides of the ships, we were a happy bunch, heading toward paradise. In the midst of that all came the blast of the ship's speaker: "NOW HEAR THIS! NOW HEAR THIS! PEARL HARBOR IS UNDER ATTACK! PEARL HARBOR IS UNDER ATTACK! WE ARE AT WAR WITH JAPAN." There was a stunned silence aboard the ship that surely we had not heard right. This could not be! Then the silence turned to fury and then grim determination.

Just like that, life changed. Our ships in the convoy began wide U-turns to steam back at full power to San Francisco. Meanwhile, the flags painted on the sides of our ships were quickly covered with oilcloth. Those flags, of which we were all proud, were like beacons to lurking submarines. All personnel were ordered top deck to watch for enemy planes and submarines. It was not something for which any of us were trained, but we quickly learned to train our eyes on the sea and sky and our ears for anything unusual. It was a tense journey back to San Francisco, so very different from the outward journey when only girls in grass skirts and drinking tall glasses of iced beer under palm trees were on our mind.

The ships were spread widely across the waves, still without escorts, with nervous troops and crew aboard. We had started out a peacetime convoy, headed to an American-friendly island paradise. We were thrust quickly into war mode. It seemed an interminable distance back, and endless time. The reality of what we suddenly faced came with the announcement that one ship in our convoy had been sunk. All on board were lost. The news that came like a ghostly wave from radio room to the watchers on deck sobered all of us. This was not an announcement boomed across the ship, but whispered in groups and read in radio messages passed from hand to hand. If there had been any question before that this was not another exercise, it was answered with all the dread and horror of war. This was real and it was terrible and people we knew would die before it was over. We looked at one another and we wondered . . . who . . . who would not return?

At that moment, at that time, photography didn't seem so important. Survival was. Still it was always at the forefront in my mind, this desire to capture forever a moment of time, a place, a person. There's a magic about photography in freezing in time an event that would never happen again quite the same. In war, there are no *do-overs*. It is that one shot, that one moment, and then the opportunity is forever gone that makes it all worthwhile. It would be four more years, but I would have that moment in time in a way I could not ever have imagined.

When we arrived back in San Francisco, there was no time to call Lucille. There was no leave. This was a serious time and personal matters were put on the back burner. I knew that I would be able to tell Lucille where I was being sent before I left. I had to. She had to be well aware that we were now at war, and she had to be worried. She couldn't know that I had returned to San Francisco, so I had to let her know. Somehow.

The 54th was dispatched to Blythe, California, for desert training. There had been no opportunity to call Lucille until I was settled in the barracks at Blythe. The relief of hearing her voice and knowing everything was all right was all I needed to get my second breath. Things were moving too swiftly.

A Co. in Blythe

From Blythe we were sent to Pomona, California, to the Los Angeles Fairgrounds, which was the designated deployment station for that area. Instead of the bright lights of a carnival atmosphere and the smell of popcorn and call of the concession hawkers, there were green tents and Army blankets spread over the concrete parking lots. Exhausted troops plopped down wherever they could. The highlight of the day was an impromptu card game. There was little talk of what awaited ahead in the vast unknown of the war overseas. For a little while, in spite of the constant reminders, the war was still far, far away.

GI's at Fairgrounds in Pomona

With only warm weather gear, light khakis, the Army lived up to its reputation of intelligence and, off we were shipped, without warning, to Iceland. No warm sleeping bags; no warm clothing; no warm parkas. My first view of Iceland was that the worse winter in the Sierras would be summer there. There were plenty of Nazi sympathizers there. The frozen land was an ideal launching place for an European invasion for the Nazis, who coveted Iceland for that reason, and now for the Allies. The Nazis were now in nearby Norway.

Iceland was a vulnerable country, and a strategic one. In area, over 39,770 square miles, it had a population back then of only 130,000 since much of its land surface was uninhabitable. There was no standing army, nor did Iceland have compulsory military service. It was a ripe plum for the picking because of its location. Although an independent state since 1918, it was England who guaranteed its independence and defense. In July of 1941, a contingent of US Marines with 4,000 men took over Iceland. Soon, there were as many Americans on the island as there were natives. It was to that small, icy cold island that I was sent in the middle of winter from sunny California.

The plan was to convince the Nazis that the invasion of Europe by the Allies would be from Iceland. Security was extremely high in Iceland as German planes flew over daily.

We lived in metal Quonset Huts, insulated somewhat from the cold by heavy bunting, strapped in place. It was primitive, but effective. We were so modern we even had our own library, complete with books, maps, and its own heating system, an ancient pot-bellied stove. There were no flushing toilets in that icy outpost; just "honey buckets" which were collected by the Icelanders and used as fertilizer on their fields in the summer.

Islandic Library

Iceland was a barren land, with no trees, no tree-lined mountains. There were scruffy hills with thick sod, and rocky, unpaved roads. The Icelanders were a hearty, ingenious people, used to the hardships of the barren land and hostile weather. They used the land, instead of fighting it. Their farmhouses often had thick, sod roofs since lumber was scarce.

Islandic Sod Covered Barn

It was my first opportunity to begin to realize my dream, there on the frozen land so unlike my homeland. I wasn't an official photographer yet, but using good old American ingenuity, I built a dark room next to the latrine, and made an enlarger from a five-gallon tin, and improvised other equipment as I needed it.

In order to have time to take my photos, I volunteered for permanent KP duty so I could have three days off, and work three. Most of the GIs were telephone and cable workers as civilians. I was kept busy taking pictures of the battalion. On pay day, the photos were sold to the guys for everyone was eager to send a photo home. Wiggins, the company clerk, handled the transactions.

My perseverance paid off, and finally the Captain and Sgt. Ferraris made me the Regimental Official Photographer. That one act in faraway Iceland set in motion the path that would lead me to Paris on May 5, 1945. One doesn't know when taking a step how important it would eventually be. I look back now and I know that the Captain could have made me shut down that dark room and even disciplined me for having it. If he had, my life would have most certainly been vastly different and the moments in time I have had the fortune to see and capture in my lens I would not have seen.

It was a small unit, but I started working in a real dark room and was happy to finally be doing what I'd wanted, what I had been promised by the recruiter. The photos weren't landscapes and personnel happily at work. These were wartime photos of things which I cannot even now describe. Along with them, I was able to photograph the people of Iceland and the unique and sometimes haunting images of the nature of Iceland. So it was that I begin my career as an official Army photographer.

Military parade in Iceland

It was still a long ways to that plaza in Paris, but as the war stretched on in Europe, I was unknowingly edging ever closer.

From Iceland, to England. At an airfield in England. My assignment was to cover the bombers returning from raid over Germany. It was not a very good sight to see the damaged planes return and some of the crew being removed lifeless from the flying fortresses. As the planes came in, I held my breath and said a prayer. Those guys in the planes were real heroes. When some were given a pass to London, they would have one hell of a time and rightly deserved, glad to be alive.

While waiting for the planes to return, I tried to cover some of the chrome on my Speed Graphic 4x5 camera. It was a real target if I got near any enemy. A fellow photographer came up to me and said he was to fly with a plane to deliver supplies to some troops. "It will be nice." He said, "as they will open a side door so we can photos on the drop. Why don't you come along?" I told him not this time as I was working on my camera. He was the nicest guy from New York. He left on the plane but never returned. He was shot down somewhere

9

in France. It shook me to think how close I had come, and I never again took another day for granted. I can still see his smile that day, and hear his voice coaxing me to go along. It was the price of war and reminder that even a photographer was at risk. Enemy fire did not discriminate.

One of my buddies, Sgt Frank Kaye, volunteered for the Normandy Invasion on D-Day. He had a 35mm camera and a small cage of trained pigeons on his back during the landing. Upon landing, with a roll of film attached to the pigeon, he sent the birds off to London. No way. The pigeons were never trained to fly over water, so he watched helplessly as they flew back in the direction of Germany, not over the English Channel. I think Frank was never the same after that snafu. I always wondered if the Germans developed his film.

That wasn't the only time that I wondered if I had a personal angel watching over me. It was not long after the plane incident that I left my billet to walk several blocks for breakfast. What greeted me was a gaping, smoldering hole where the dining room and kitchen were. A V-1 rocket had hit it, taking with it the staff and the GIs gathering for breakfast. If I had been on time . . . I tried not to think of that as I stood in horror, watching the smoke rise, and listening to the sirens. That is the kind of picture that lingers in the mind.

While in Salisbury, the editor of the local paper asked if someone could take some photos for the paper as the Dutchess of Kent would be visiting Salisbury. The paper had managed to stay in business, but its photographer had been lost to the war. It was another slice of fortune for me, and I was in the right place at the right time. I made some points there, and the general's public relation's man, Lt. Berger, wrote me a nice commendation.

Dutchess of Kent

Soon after that event, I got my transfer to London. The Army Pictorial Service (Army Signal Corps). After all the kicking around, London was like heaven. We were billeted in some nice quarters with good chow. My company commander was Major McAlister, and his secretary Virginia, who was a WAC (Women's Army Corp). We were given assignments and sent all over Europe, sometimes by plane or jeep.

In London, dodging buzz bombs was as routine as walking on the beach in Seaside, California, during basic training at Ft. Ord. At least, I was where I wanted to be, and doing my photography. I was in London about eight months when I had the privilege of photographing the Queen of England. She wasn't the least bit standoffish or elitist. I was surprised that she was pleasant to me, a foreign Army photographer. I talked to Her Majesty and told her about California. It was a great time at Badminton Palace.

Badminton Palace with Queen Mom

One other assignment was the coverage of V-2 rocket that landed outside of London, leaving a huge crater and damaging many homes. Highly secret, the papers said that a gas main had exploded. After that, several crates arrived from Sweden and I photographed the many parts. The civilian with whom I was working told me they are trying to find where the parts are made so they could bomb the factory and hold up production on the bomb. They were placed each piece over a large framework and I carefully photographed the pieces from all angles.

Doodle bug trap

On one of my walks around, with the sound of a V-1 on its way, I decided to run for cover under the Metro. Next to me was a lovely young redhead. I made a date to meet her the following night at the theatre where she was in the stage play. Of course, I was thinking of Lucy back home, but it would be nice to talk to someone other than the Dog Faces. I went to meet her at the theatre, but a terrible sight greeted me. There was nothing but jagged bricks and torn curtains and broken glass. The whole theatre and the cast were killed the night before by a V-1 rocket. What a crime, and one I will never forget!

V-1 rocket aftermath

On one assignment, a colonel from a general's office on ordinance, we had to go to Holland and check on the artillery and take photos of the British hardware. The colonel loved to get out in the fields and be a soldier. He drove the jeep. We were heading for Holland and it was raining heavily. He hit some guy on a bike, but kept going. Don't know how he made it. Later on, we picked up a Brit who was hiking.

The colonel told me to sit in the back of the jeep and he would tell the Brit I was a Lieutenant. He said otherwise they would not accept us. The Brit Captain invited us to their regimental headquarters for dinner. Of course, I had to sit next to an officier at this huge dinner table. This guy kept asking me about our artillery as my colonel told them we were from ordinance. "Poor dumb sot," he must have thought as I didn't know the difference between a sling-shot and a bee-bee gun. He probably thought, "How these chaps ever made it over here, I wouldn't know."

One night we slept in a hay barn, and the colonel loved it as he could play soldier. As for me, I wanted back to London and a nice, warm sack. We were all living in some nice apartment. It was not that way, always. In spite of the accommodations, there was no question but what we were in the middle of a war. The nightly bombings continued; black curtains were drawn across every window, and sirens blasted throughout the night. I would have gladly given up the faux luxury to be back home with Lucille.

Finally, the outfit got orders to ship off to France, and I did not know it at the time, but I was on the last leg of my journey to the Plaza de la Concorde. Fates were set in motion for that one moment in time when history would unfold in front of my lens. While the Nazi presence wasn't as pronounced as it had been, there were still signs that they had been there and always the threat that they would return. The French weren't convinced that the Nazis were gone. The war still went on, and the echo of the bombs stayed with them, even if the sound was only in memory. It was not a memory anyone wanted repeated. There was an uneasiness about Paris that superseded any pleasure of being there.

The Battalion was set up in the heart of Paris. Our living quarters were nothing like regular Army. It was a beautiful apartment with maid service to make up our beds. I was on the third floor, and rarely did the maid make it up there, especially if she was good looking. The Rothchilds Mansion was just a block away, an example of the fancy area we were in. Just as in England, the luxury did not hide the scars of war or the fact that the war was still ablaze all around us.

At our office, five of us waited for assignments. As we got an assignment. Major McAlistre's secretary, Virginia, made all the arrangements, such as transportation and length of time to do the job. If you were nice to Virginia, she would tack on a few extra days. It was great so when you got back, you needed not report until your time was up. It was great to run around Paris and act like a civilian. The populace were very friendly and would pay anything for a pack of American cigarettes. Each week, we were allowed a carton of cigarettes at the Post Exchange and couldn't get a block before the cigarettes were sold. The French had plenty of money with nothing to buy.

One incident which really lingers was a truck load of war-weary and dirty GIs arrived at the Red Cross for recreation and showers, which they probably had not had for weeks. The word got out to some of the brass. "Hell, we can't have these dirty guys in Paris. (bad image)." So back to the trucks and return to wherever they came from. No showers. No nothing. I can still feel their frustration. I suppose the officer of that group really got chewed out for allowing the "dirty warriors" to arrive in Paris.

Another assignment was to go to Gen. Lears' headquarters on several photo jobs. He lived in a Chateau several miles out of Paris and rather hard to find. The general was a hot potato. All San Francisco, California, papers had the headline, "Yoo-hoo Lear." It was possible that Gen. Eisenhower wanted him out of sight. The reason back in the states a military convoy was passing a golf course here in California. As the convoy loaded with troop were yelling "Yoo-hoo" at the foursome and one in the group was wearing knickers. Of course, the troops did not know it was Gen. Lear. The general found out which outfit did that dastardly thing and had them, do a ten-mile hike with a full pack.

Maj. McAllister wanted me to report right away as Gen. Lear was giving an award to Gen. Bonsteel, who was the commander of the Iceland Base. The Major said I was the only one who knew how to find the Chateau.

I had an assignment to travel with some of the US senators, House Military Committee. We traveled all over France. A full Colonel was escorting them as he was from the Washington Chief of Staff. On one of the stops was a visit to Hitler's Berchtesgaden. The place was guarded by many Military Police. As we visited the Hitler library, I helped myself to two first edition books and put them in my camera case. While flying on the plane, I was looking at my treasures. The colonel in the next aisle said, "Sergeant, I sure would like one of those books." I thought, play it safe, and offered him one. He said he would write to my folks and tell them I was okay. He did that, and I heard later he was coming out of the Paris Hotel, slipped and broke a leg. Purple heart for sure.

The war was still going on. My assignment to join the 82nd Airborne on a glider drop into Holland. I was at the English airfield and briefed on where we were to land. Three times, I sat in the glider, but each flight was aborted due to bad weather. I called the Major and he said to come in. I left in a jeep, and the next day the invasion took place. It was a disaster with ninety-percent casualties. The object was the capture of the Ramagen Bridge. I was lucky on that one. My angel was still with me.

Not too much later, I was sent with a movie man, Herb Shannon. We were to report with the 82nd Airborne as the Battle of the Bulge had started. We were pretty much on our own. We latched up with regimental headquarters. We ended up in a small, deserted village in France. Everyone had left, so we had our choice of houses. It was December and very cold. Winter in France took second place only to winter in Iceland. We picked a house and put our sleeping bags upstairs for the night. In the morning, we grabbed our mess kits and headed for the field kitchen. Help! The whole regiment moved out during the night. There we were on our own, with the Germans on the march in our direction. I fancied I could hear the German regiment. I was positive they were out there, right beyond the edge of the trees. Shannon and I hurried out of there, looking over our shoulders at every sound, expecting at any moment to hear a German voice shouting, HALT! We finally followed the track in the mud and caught up with the Regiment.

While covering the front line, I was able to get a good photo of one of the 82nd guys running to help his buddy as the Germans were firing at us. In that exchange, several of the enemy were killed and no one on our side was killed or injured. It had been about a week, terribly cold and I was dreaming about Paris. Finally, a new lieutenant from Headquarters found us. "Been trying to find you guys. I have a message, and you guys are to report to Eagle."

Soldier running

Battle of the Bulge; downed plane

I knew this guy did not know about Eagle. Great! Eagle was the code name for Paris. "Well, if you guys say so." We jumped in our jeep and off to Paris we went.

We reported to Major McAlister in Paris. "What are you guys doing here?"

"Lt Sheldon told us to return." We found out later Eagle was not Paris but the 10th Army Corps Headquarters. I always felt rather bad. We no doubt got the lieutenant in trouble.

In retrospect, it's strange how pieces of fate fell into place so I was in the right place at the right time, and on May 8, 1945, I stood in the Plaza de la Concorde and swept my camera over the gathering crowd. At precisely 3:01 Pacific War Time, General deGaulle's voice came over the loud speakers from the opera house. "The war in Europe is ended. Germany has surrendered. Viva la France." And so began this photographic memoir of victory Europe as seen from the streets of Paris, France.

Eiffel Tower 1945: Easily, the most recognizable monument of Paris, France. In spite of its ordered destruction, the Eiffel Tower was saved by an unlikely champion. Nazi Major General Dietrich von Choltitz went against a direct order from Hitler and refused to set off explosives attached to the famed Tower. The Major General, who had been the occupying governor of Paris during the German Occupation, had been informed by Hitler that Paris was on direct path of liberation, and he was ordered to destroy everything, burn Paris to the ground, and leave nothing but scorched earth and smoldering bodies in his wake. General von Choltitz was not a stranger to this policy, having carried it out in manufacturing and farm towns in Russia. In his final meeting with Hitler, he had been ordered to level Paris and "stamp out without pity" all life there, rather than have it fall to the liberators. Von Choltitz was instructed to personally see that every major monument, including the Eiffel Tower, the Arch of Triumph and the Cathedral at Norte Dame, were utterly destroyed. Explosives were deployed throughout the city, and in the tunnels under Paris, U-boat torpedoes waited to be ignited. The General was convinced by his final meeting with Hitler that his Fuehrer was a madman and there was no military or political advantage in burning Paris. He did not want his final legacy to be of the man who destroyed Paris. His defiance cost him his career and his liberty. In August, 1944, General Dietrich von Choltitz surrendered Paris, defying Hitler for the only time during his career. The Parisians who spat on him as he was led away by thirty armed guards of the liberators of Paris were unaware that he was the savior of not only the magnificent Eiffel Tower, but also all of Paris, its people, and its historical and irreplaceable treasures.

3:01 P.M. Pacific War Time – Opera Bastille – Paris – May 5, 1945: At precisely 3:01 p.m. Pacific War Time, the voice of French General deGaulle boomed over the speakers mounted on the outside of the opera house. **"The war in Europe is ended. Germany has surrendered. Viva la France."** The Plaza filled with cheering Parisians, French and American soldiers. Within five minutes of the announcement there were shoulder-to-shoulder celebrants, standing on every edifice and shouting from every rooftop. Note the clock in the right hand corner of this photograph, which records the exact moment.

The Celebration Reached the Arc de Triomphe (Arch of Triumph): They kept coming until it seemed every citizen of France, every Allied soldier; every American in Paris filled the Plaza de la Concorde from the Opera House to the Arch de Triumph and onward. In this photograph, the Arc de Triomphe can just be seen at the end of the Plaza. Napoleon had it commissioned in 1806 after the victory at Austerlitz. At the end of the World War II in Europe, it once again became a symbol of victory for the Parisians.

Grand Hotel – Paris, France -- May 5, 1945: The cheering crowd in the Plaza spilled around to the Grand Hotel which faced a corner of the Plaza. Note the American soldiers on top of a lamppost and the exuberant people looking up at them. In the crowd is a mixture of French civilians, and French and American soldiers. In spite of the earlier liberation of Paris, Parsians did not feel fully free or at liberty to assemble until the announcement by General deGaulle.

Traffic at a Standstill: At the time of the liberation of Paris, there were still a few gasoline powered vehicles, but gas was strictly rationed and so only the elite had automobiles. When General deGualle announced the end of the war, those few automobiles clogged the Plaza with the honking of their horns. It was impossible for them to move and so people took advantage of yet another place to stand and be heard. None of those cars made it out of the Plaza unscratched, but no one cared. The War was over! France was free once more!

Arc de' Triomphe (Arch of Triumph): The arch was commissioned by Napoleon in 1806 to commemorate his victories, but he was ousted before the arch was completed. In fact, it wasn't completed until 1836 during the reign of Louis-Philippe. The Arc de Triomphe is engraved with names of generals who commanded French troops during Napoleon's regime. It was slated for destruction by an angry Hitler who ordered his occupying General Choltitz to set off explosives on, under and around it. The General refused to do Hitler's last bidding. Below is a picture of the Arch prior to the announcement of the war's end. Note that horse drawn carriages were the mode of transportation as gas was scarce.

Arc de Triomphe on May 5, 1945: The long days of occupation and dread were over. The City of Light was once again free, and the French and Americans could not contain their cheering. An endless stream of people flowed out from the Plaza de la Concorde down the twelve streets above which it towers. As the day progressed, more and more people came to share the celebration. Imagine, if you will, having been under Nazi control and then freed.

"V" for Victory at the Arc de' Triomphe: There was no containing the populace! They ran; they walked; they climbed on military vehicles, and they gave the "V" for victory sign to everyone. The two flags said it all: French and American, symbols of the victory and the freedom won at last. The military vehicle on which is a pyramid of people is an American evacuation truck, which purpose was to take civilians and injured troops out of harm's way. This time it served a much more joyful purpose. The driver couldn't see where he was going, but he didn't care! Forward to victory!

Military Construction Truck and Human Cargo: Under all of those people, who clung to the sides, tires, bed, and cab was a heavy duty military construction truck, originally in France to clear debris and rebuild damaged roads and bridges. Men, women, youth, children clung to every inch of the vehicle as it slowly moved toward the Plaza. Its forward pace was halted by the weight and amount of people. In spite of the surging crowd, the American flag was left unmolested.

American Soldiers Share the Victory: Not too long before, this military jeep and the ambulance beside it were at the front lines in a road to battle. Now, they shared a different purpose. The jeep driver was signaling at me that there was room for more.

Youth of Paris: In the days of the occupation, France's youth couldn't attend college, and many were pressed into service. Even after the liberation of Paris, their futures were unsure. It wasn't until the war in Europe was officially over that these young men and women could express their exuberance, as they did here. Note the sign *"les Js A Berlin."* This was in reference to the Soviet's Tiger Tanks (JS-3) rolling into Berlin.

Virginia: Virginia was the secretary to Major McAlister, who was head of the Army Signal Corps in Paris. She was a hard worker who gave us photographers our assignments. She put up with a lot, and when the war was declared over, she took what I considered her rightful place on a pedestal. Note the clock on the court building. This is less than one hour after the declaration by deGaulle.

Virginia and Friend: We couldn't let Virginia stand there all by herself! This GI saw Virginia standing there and had to join her.

General deGaulle Awarding Medals: When Paris was liberated nine months before the war ended, Eisenhower let General deGaulle enter Paris before the American troops, out of courtesy to the French people and their general. The fighting still raged in Europe after the liberation of Paris. Even parts of France were not completely free. It wasn't until May 5, 1945, that Parisians could breathe freely. General deGaulle, after making his announcement, awarded medals to both his French legions and his American allies. Here he is pinning *the Legion of Honor* on Lt. General Walter B. Smith, Supreme Commanders' Chief of Staff. The Allied Supreme Commander, General Dwight D. Eisenhower, is in the foreground.

General Dwight Eisenhower, Supreme Commander: Every military and civilian photographer from miles around came for this event! It wasn't every day one could see and photograph the Supreme Commander of the Allied Forces in Europe. General deGaulle is seen here pinning France's higherst honor, the Legion of Honor medal, on General Eisenhower.

General Eisenhower: General Charles deGaulle, leader of the French resistance against Nazi Germany, bestows the "Fellow of the Liberation" award on General Dwight Eisenhower, Commander of the Allied Forces, which liberated France. General Eisenhower had insisted that General deGaulle be first into Paris upon the liberation.

General Eisenhower shaking hands with General Patton: During his tour of the Western Front, General Dwight D. Eisenhower, Supreme Allied Commander, shakes hands with Lt. General George S. Patton of the 3rd Army, as they depart from Bastogne. Lt. General Omar N. Bradley, CG, 12th Army GP, looks on. General Eisenhower highly praised the defenders of the historic city.

General Eisenhower and General Giraud: General Eisenhower shaking hands with French General Giraud after the awarding of the Fellow of the Liberation medal. This was one of my favorite photographs. General Eisenhower was a hero to all of us.

Emil Snatched by the Police: Shortly after I took the above photograph, this one was taken by a fellow photographer. That's me, just behind General Eisenhower being pulled backed by a French Gendaramerie (Policeman). He told me I had already a picture and to get back.

General Eisenhower and General deGaulle: General Eisenhower shaking hands with General deGaulle at the end of the ceremonies. During the war, General Eisenhower and General deGaulle were at odds many times. But at this moment, when the war in Europe was over and the formal ceremonies had ended, the French and American Generals were all smiles. Their goal had always been the same: liberation of Europe.

Deuil National en France Pour la Mort de Roosevelt: President Roosevelt did not live to see the end of the war in Europe. He died on April 12, 1945, less than a month before the announcement that the war was over. In liberated France, but not yet Nazi-free, taxi drivers read the headlines announcing the death of the American President. The headline reads, *"National mourning in France for the death of Roosevelt."* These taxi drivers are sitting in a *velocab*, developed during the occupation. These cabs were constructed of a loose frame where seats were and were pulled by a bicycle. They were an innovation due to lack of gasoline. Note in the newspaper, upper right, there is a picture of Roosevelt and Truman. On the left-hand side is the swearing-in of Truman.

France Citizen Reads of Roosevelt's Death: The Frenchman on the bench is absorbed in reading about Roosevelt's death. The woman in the center is oblivious and is, instead, enjoying a book on that cool, spring morning.

Gargoyles on Roof of Notre Dame Cathedral: This legendary cathedral, "Our Lady of Paris," was originally built in 1163, commissioned by Bishop Maurice de Sully. It was to be a monument to Paris as the center of the Kingdom of France. It took until 1345 to be completed. The gargoyles were used generously throughout the edifice and roof. Mixed with angels, these Gothic sculptures were thought to scare away evil spirits. During World War II, some of the priceless stained glass windows were removed in fear of being destroyed by Nazi bombs. The famous cathedral owes its survival to German General Dietrich von Choltiz.

Cherub Looking Toward Bonaparte's Tomb: On the bride of Pont des Invalides, cherubs protects all who walk there. The old lamps along the pathway were originally gas lamps, lit by a lamplighter each evening. They are now electric, but still reflect that candle-light ambiance.

French Soldiers Marching Toward Church of Saint Louis: After the war's end, French Soldiers march up the road toward the Church of Saint Louis for a ceremony at the tomb of Emperor Bonaparte. In spite of his ultimate defeat, Bonaparte is considered one of France's most revered heroes. This church and the Emperor's tomb were spared destruction by Hitler who admired Napoleon.

Pedal Power: With the war over, celebrations behind them, Paris slowly tried to return to normal. There still was a great gasoline shortage. Bikes were no longer just transportation for children. It became the preferred method of travel for everyone, include merchants, workers, and delivery people. Notice the absence of gasoline vehicles on these wide, cobblestone streets.

Following the official end of the war, there was an overwhelming need to honor the war dead, including the many civilians who fell victim to bombs or the atrocities of war. The woman with the flowers is delivering a wreath and a bouquet to a cemetery.

I was curious about this man in as I wondered how he could see where he was going. I never found out where he was delivering the large floral arrangements, but because of the lilies, I wondered if he, too, was heading for the cemetery. In the City of Romance, more floral tributes were to the dead than to enhance romance.

Pedal Power: While there were cars, there was little, precious gasoline to fuel them. The bicycle became the transportation of the moment for a wide variety of people.

This woman caught my attention because she obviously didn't like her picture taken. She gave me a rather familiar "salute." Parisians were good at adapting to whatever life handed them. She left me to wonder what she did, or didn't do, during the war that prompted such a response from an American photographer.

Of all the bicycles around Paris that day, this one caught my attention because of poodle riding on the back. The dog is not secured, but riding there as though he had been on that seat all of his life. He probably had. It was surprising to me that so many dogs survived the war because of rationing of food.

Horse Power: Joining the bicycle as transportation was the horse. Horses were both individual transportation and business ventures. The horse and carriage was the elite form of transportation. There were still no gas-driven vehicles in the large plaza. While there were cars, there was no gasoline to power them.

These two women are an interesting study in contrast, with one on a bicycle and one on a horse. They almost seemed as though they were racing each other. A horse downtown Paris was not an unusual sight.

The Surrey: In this photo, a horse pulls a surrey, or pony cart with three rather elegant looking Parisians. Before the war, this type of transportation was for romantic nights in the City of Light. Right after the war, the surrey was transformed from a whimsical evening on the town to a necessary form of getting around.

Motorbike: This couple was a study in what it meant to be in liberated Paris. This small motor scooter had the double power of pedal and a small amount of gasoline. This couple has their poodle and wine had the street all to themselves. The buildings on either side are empty and closed stores. There are two abandoned automobiles down by the curve, a reminder of how busy that cobblestone street once was. Note the tracks in the street. A commuter train once ran down this street when it was a busy and thriving community. I always wondered where this couple was heading down that lonely road on their own private journey to celebrate the end of the war.

Merchants of Paris: The stores had been stripped of their merchandise during the occupation. In the year that followed, Parisians did whatever they could to survive. Street merchants were the norm instead of the exception. Many did not have a horse or a bicycle to peddle their wares, and a truck was not possible because of the scarcity of fuel. The pushcarts were a common sight in post-war Paris.

In this picture, a woman pushes a cart with bags of flowers. Note the sign on her cart that says 10¢. Many of these pushcart merchants walked all the way from the country, where the flowers were picked, pushing the heavy carts, into the City to hopefully make a sale. Although some of these flowers freshened homes, many of them ended up in the cemetery to honor the war dead.

Merchants of Paris: An old woman sits on a damaged wooden chair in front of her vegetable pushcart, as she talks to a prospective customer. There were no scales. The seller sold by quantity, not weight, gauging the amount by how it felt in her hands. The old chair was placed on top of her pushcart as she carefully treaded her way from the countryside to the streets of Paris to hawk her wares. I wondered about her, why this old woman made that long trek. She may have been either the only survivor of her family, or the only able-bodied one.

Merchants of Paris: This pushcart merchant reads a newspaper as he waits for customers. Again, this is a street merchant without visible means of transportation. He, like the women, more than likely pushed his cart from somewhere outside the city and chose this spot, in front of vacant, empty stores, to sell his ware. The woman strolling by with her pram (baby carriage) is not interested. Note, again, the absence of automobiles.

Merchants of Paris: Not everyone could afford even a pushcart, but that didn't stop them. Some walked for miles to reach the square in Paris to sell their wares. At times, that walk was so far that the vegetables brought to market were wilted. In a city that suffered hunger during the occupation, a little wilting of food didn't dissuade them.

There is such character on the face of this old woman. She had walked miles with a heavy bag of cabbage and exhaustion can clearly be seen in her weathered face. She sat on the scarred stone steps with her cabbages, patiently waiting for a buyer. She sat there all day and into the evening, selling her cabbages for what amounted to pennies a piece. I could imagine her returning to her home and having cabbage soup for supper.

Vegetable "Hat:" A definite innovative way a merchant sold her wares. No, that is not a fancy Parisian hat she's wearing, but her merchandise. From her expression, she was literally "grinning and bearing it."

Market Les Halles: This outdoor farmers market was a mainstay in all of France, especially Paris. During the occupation, agriculture was both regulated and confiscated, and the farmers market disappeared. After the liberation of Paris, the farmers market returned with zeal. These baskets were mostly carried there on the shoulders of farmers. The marking on the baskets were to identify them at the end of the day.

Merchants of Paris: In spite of their long ordeal, Parisians did not lose their self-respect. After the occupation and the liberation, the citizenry begin to reassert itself.

In the first picture, the master of the house, used to having his man-servant do his shopping, found himself in a personal barter with the street vendor. Note the American soldiers in the background, looking on.

In the second picture, this craftsman caught my attention as he sat on the curb, repairing broken dishes. The tools of his trade on the street in front of him, he carefully pieced together crockery and sealed it. He seemed oblivious of everything and everyone around him

Women of Paris: There were many shortages during and after the war, but there were no shortage of beautiful women in Paris. They weren't shy about having their photographs taken, either. The young lady in the first photograph is posing in front of bronze horses' head in Paris. The writing on the pedestal states: *Alexis Rudier Fonderie Paris*. This was the largest foundry in France and *The Thinker* by Auguste Rodin was cast there. *The Horses' Head* was a classic example of that expertise. Many of Paris' art treasures were looted during the occupation, but this statue was so large it was left alone.

Women of Paris: This blonde caught my attention, not only because of her natural beauty but also because she was walking a poodle. Poodles and Paris always seem to go together, yet the favorite dog of Paris in the 1940s were the larger breeds who provided protection. The poodle came into its own after the war. Note the vehicle behind her is an Army jeep, the only vehicles which had access to petro.

Art of Paris: Paris, the City of Light, has always been famous for its art and artisans. Although much of Paris' art was plundered by the Nazis, and many of its renowned artists fled, such as Pablo Picasso and Carlos Casagemas, many more stayed. There were two very widely different types of artists in Paris during, and right after, the war.

Hitler, a brutal dictator and a man without conscience, had a strange affinity for the arts. He had, at one time, aspirations of being an artist himself, which might explain why he spared this gallery the destruction wreaked upon so many other historical places. After the war, patrons begin returning, and I caught these in my camera's eye, walking through the gallery as though this pleasure had never been interrupted by war.

Gypsies of Paris: This is an example of a very different, but equally interesting, type of artist, the Gypsy. Gypsies were actively prosecuted by the Nazis during World War II, forced into "relocation camps" (aka concentration camps), and either literally worked to death or summarily executed. Those who were fortunate enough to escape before the Nazi roundup gradually returned to France after the liberation of Paris. The sign on the trailer announces: *"Revelation du Destin - Choisier le mois – de voltre naissance cette Dame connais tous."* This is the home of a Gypsy fortune teller who promises: "Revelation of Destiny – This Lady Knows All."

Religion of Paris: Religion has always played an important role in Paris. The prominent religion was Catholic, and the most famous of the churches were St. Louis Cathedral and Notre Dame Cathedral. That the churches were spared is again because of General Dietrich von Choltitz. Although he can be credited with refusal to destroy Paris' architectural treasures, including its cathedrals, the general was not a hero to be revered.

What I found interesting in this photo is the peacefulness of the two nuns who did not know they were being photographed. Although there is much controversy about the role the Catholic Church played during the occupation, Catholics was still the primary religion for France and the men and women of the cloth were revered. There were many nuns who worked tirelessly during the War to help the underground, as well as others who defied the Nazis and the occupation.

Priests of Paris: This priest walking the street, paid no attention to anyone around him as he reads passages out of the Bible. In the background there are American soldiers enjoying the warm day as the priest walks by. Throughout the occupation, many priests walked a tightrope, outwardly portraying themselves as neutral to prevent their imprisonment or even execution by the Germans, while at the same time helping the Resistance. There's no way to know if the priest in this picture was one of them, but he caught my eye because of his concentration on the Bible, and oblivion to those around him.

The last photograph is of a Catholic man of the cloth showing his papers to a French policeman. Even after the war was over, there were still the requirement to show one's papers. Many Germans disguised themselves as civilians, or even men of the cloth, to escape persecution.

Homeward Bound: This group of American GIs are waiting to debark France for home. There was both a joyful anticipation of being in the States again as well as a somber farewell. Almost all of these men began their enlistment as teenagers, and left France as seasoned veterans, old before their time. I have often wondered what happened to the men who attended this impromptu concert and the accordionist who provided the music.

The Call Bulletin, 31 June 1955, President Eisenhower, after addressing UN in San Francisco. Photo taken by Emil who was remembered by Ike and given a warm welcome.

Bulganin Vows Peace Try | TODAY'S N. Y. STOCKS

TENSIONS EASING, BRITON TELLS UN

'SO LONG, SAN FRANCISCO'
With a jaunty wave of his hat, a beaming President Eisenhower says goodbye to San Francisco after addressing the UN meeting here. Snapping a smart salute is St. Francis Hotel doorman Charley Bristol. (Full page of UN photos, Page 19.)—Call-Bulletin Photo by Emil Edgren

The Call Bulletin

THE CALL BULLETIN VOL. 191, NO. 141
CALL AND POST   VOL. 173, NO. 141

TUESDAY, JUNE 21, 1955   10c DAILY

Parley Of Big 4 Ministers Ends On Amity Note

UN SESSION
Tensions Easing— Macmillan

By HUBERT J. BERNHARD
Call-Bulletin Staff Writer

Four weary but still-smiling foreign ministers finished a long conference atop Nob Hill early today—with peace, apparently, uppermost in their minds.

It was peace, as envisioned in a proposed "San Francisco Declaration" to be made before the United Nations, and suggested first by Soviet Minister

Other UN News and Photos
On Pages 2, 3, 6, 7 and 19

WEATHER

Bay Area—Fair today, tonight and tomorrow, but high fog on coast extending inland in mornings. High today, San Francisco 64, Oakland 68, San Mateo 64.

By JANE ESHLEMAN CONANT
Call-Bulletin Staff Writer

British Foreign Secretary Harold Macmillan told the United Nations today that the seemingly unending tensions between East and West are easing.

And the great powers can get back on the road of co-operation, he declared, "if we can apply the big pioneering spirit to the work that lies before

CPSIA information can be obtained
at www.ICGtesting.com
Printed in the USA
BVHW020235081019
560463BV00002B/2/P